Written by Ronald J. Schlegel
Illustrated by Jim Roberts

A Garden and a Promise

Genesis 1—3 FOR CHILDREN

© 1973 All rights reserved.
CONCORDIA PUBLISHING HOUSE LTD.,
117/123 Golden Lane, London EC1Y OTL.
Printed in England.

ISBN 0-570-06072-9

Publishing House
St. Louis London

Before there were roses or dandelions or trees,
giraffes or dogs or chimpanzees;
when man did not as yet exist
and earth was watered by a mist,

God took some specks of dust He found
just lying there upon the ground;
He shaped the dust and formed a man
and breathed into his nose, and then

the man could walk and talk and sing,
for he was now a living thing!

God saw the man that He had made.
"That's very good," the Lord God said,
"I'll make him plants for food, and see—
animals for company!"

Then God told the man, "Every plant in view
I give you to be food for you,
except the tree of knowledge of good
and evil; that one's not for food!"
So the man ate the fruit from the rest of the trees
and lived quite a while contentedly.

But after awhile God said to the man,
"You're all alone, so now I plan
to find a helper fit for you;
I'm sure that won't be hard to do."

Then God told the animals He had made
to form an animal parade
and walk past the man one by one,
and the man said,
"Say, this sure is fun.

Look at that animal hopping by,
I really couldn't tell you why
I want to call it what I do,
but it looks to me like a *kangaroo*!"

Of all the animals he spoke much the same,
and whatever he called one, that was its name:
lion—hippopotamus—elephant—bear;
but among them all not anywhere

was a helper found fit for the man.
So God said, "I've a different plan.
I'll put you to sleep for an hour or two
and *make* a helper fit for you."

Then God made a woman from the rib He'd taken from the man, and when the man awakened, the man looked at her and said, "Finally, I have a helper fit for me!

"I'll call her 'woman,' for she alone is flesh of my flesh and bone of my bone!"

So the man and woman lived happily
eating fruit from every tree
that God had given, except the one
from which God had said it should not be done.

Then one day, when the woman was walking alone among the trees, she heard the drone of the voice of the snake, saying, "Did God really say you shouldn't eat the fruit? How silly!"

"We may eat it all," the woman said,
and then she added with a nod of her head,
"We may eat of all the trees except one;
of that tree in the centre we must eat none,
or we'll surely die; so God has said,
and we sure don't wish to end up dead!"

"You will not die," the snake replied;
"rather God knows that when you've tried
that fruit, your eyes will open far,
and you'll know what good and evil are!"

The woman looked at the fruit in surprise,
and for the first time she realized
that *that* fruit looked better than any
   of the other;
so she picked one, then picked another.

The one she ate. The other she shared
with the man; very soon they became quite scared,
for the fruit indeed had made them wise
to good and evil — it opened their eyes;
and soon they began to feel quite bad

and very ashamed of the bodies they had,
so (since they didn't have cloth or leather)
they gathered some fig leaves and sewed them
together

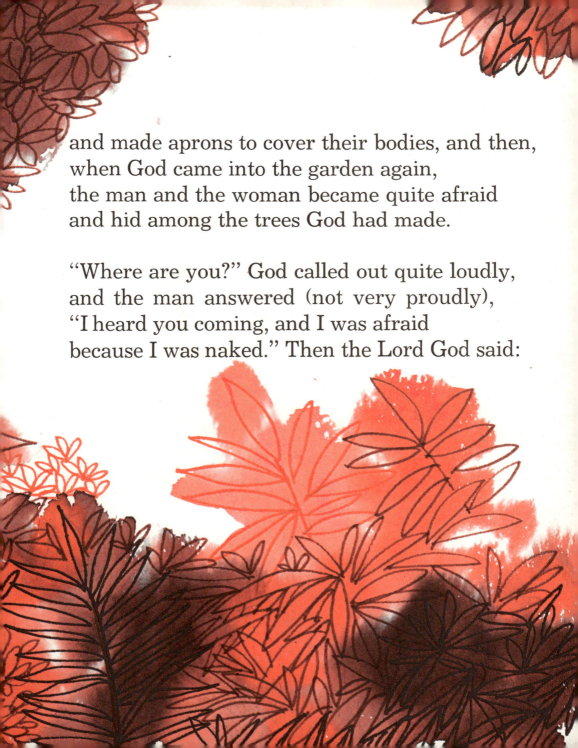

and made aprons to cover their bodies, and then,
when God came into the garden again,
the man and the woman became quite afraid
and hid among the trees God had made.

"Where are you?" God called out quite loudly,
and the man answered (not very proudly),
"I heard you coming, and I was afraid
because I was naked." Then the Lord God said:

"Who said you were naked? Why have you hid? Have you eaten the fruit that I forbid?"

The man replied, "The woman You made brought me the fruit." The woman said, "It wasn't my fault, it was the snake who made me do it, for goodness' sake!"

Then God said, "Because of what you have done
your lives will be different from this moment on.
You, snake, will crawl on the ground through the
    dust.
And as for you, man, from now on you must
work hard for your food and for clothes to put on."
Then to the woman God said, "Because of what
    you have done
You will have pain and sorrow too;
but one day I promise I'll rescue you
from sin and death, so you never need fear,
for I'll be with you always, year after year."

So the man and the woman were driven away
from their beautiful home in the garden that day,
the day they decided they wanted to be
like God and ate from the forbidden tree.

But God promised them that one day He'd send
His Son down to earth to rescue all men
from their terrible fate, and He promised He'd
   never
leave them but that He'd be with them forever.

DEAR PARENTS:

Nice as solitude is sometimes, prolonged isolation from others often leads to severe illness, mental or physical or both. People just tend to be happiest when they're with other people. So God made Eve for Adam, and they enjoyed exploring the world together.

Together, too, they did a terrible thing. They decided they could be like God if they ate the forbidden fruit. They ate it and unleashed sin and death for all generations. God had warned them, but they didn't believe Him. They didn't trust Him.

Now they knew the greatest isolation of all. They no longer felt together with God. To live in that awful isolation for long would certainly mean death. But God still loved His creatures. He reached out to them and bound them to Himself again with a promise.

We have seen that promise fulfilled. We know now that because God sent His Son, we have togetherness with Him and with each other forever.

As you discuss the story with the child, draw on his own experiences of loneliness and togetherness.

THE EDITOR